TEXT BY **ANNIE KELLY**

PHOTOGRAPHY BY TIM STREET-PORTER

RIZZOLI
NEW YORK

New York Paris London Milan

SPLASH

THE ART OF THE SWIMMING POOL

Dedicated to the late tropical landscape designer Made Wijaya
as well as the late bamboo pioneer Linda Garland. We would also like
to dedicate this book to our long-term swimming pool–owning
friends and designers, including Florence de Dampierre,
Matthew Rolston, Ted Russell, Manolo Mestre, Martyn Lawrence Bullard,
Barry Sloane, and Isabel Goldsmith.

TABLE OF CONTENTS

Introduction 8

GARDEN POOLS
Landscaping Oases 16

ARCHITECTURAL POOLS
Integrated Swimming Pools 76

INFINITY POOLS
The Vanishing Edge 118

FANTASY POOLS
Creating Dreams 144

POOL ELEMENTS 176
Spas and Outdoor Showers 177
Steps 192
Edging 196
Pool Houses 200
Furnishings 212

Acknowledgments 222

INTRODUCTION

Water. We can't get enough of it. We swim in it, drink it, and bathe in it. It reflects the sky in its purity, and inspires peace and tranquility. A swimming pool has become an integral part of a home, extending the usable space into a garden. It can be designed to mirror the architecture of the house or act as a destination point elsewhere on the property. Swimming pools have become so popular over the last fifty years, with one in almost every suburban backyard, that it is easy to forget that their documented origin goes back over five thousand years.

While people have been bathing since humankind's first discovery of rock pools, the Great Bath at the site of Mohenjo-Daro in modern-day Pakistan was most likely the first recorded swimming pool. Dug during the third millennium BCE, this pool was lined with hand-cut blocks of stone and covered with a tar-based sealant.

Both the ancient Greeks and Romans built artificial pools for athletic training and health reasons. A fresco, from around 470 BCE, discovered in the Tomba del Tuffatore in Greece shows a remarkably modern-looking depiction of a figure leaping into water from a diving board. Roman emperors enjoyed private swimming pools in which fish were also kept; hence one of the Latin words for a pool is *piscina*. These were decorated with columns and statues, and included colorful wall frescos and mosaics. The first documented heated swimming pool was built in Rome in the first century BCE. Roman

enthusiasm for pools spread across the empire—they could be found from Hadrian's Villa near Rome to the town of Pompeii, and they became an accoutrement that spread to France and Germany as well as in the famous town of Bath in England.

In Asia, the Sinhalese built a pair of pools called Kuttam Pokuna in the kingdom of Anuradhapura, Sri Lanka, in the fourth century BCE, while in China, the Huaqing hot springs at the foot of Mount Lishan have been in continuous use for over three thousand years.

In Latin America, Inca palaces were built near natural geothermal ponds, while cenotes in Mexico, deep natural

OPPOSITE: The author admiring the ocean view from the Post Ranch Inn infinity pool in California's Big Sur. ABOVE: A fresco at the Tomba del Tuffatore in Greece from around 470 BCE.

pools of water used for ceremonial purposes, were used for centuries to bathe in as well as being a convenient ceremonial repository for gold and jewels.

After the fall of the Roman Empire, the popularity of swimming pools waned as regular bathing became uncommon in Europe for many hundreds of years until the fashion revived in the 1700s. At that time, docks were added to European rivers to help with the new fashion of bathing in the summer.

However, the real resurgence occurred when swimming became a competitive sport at the newly reestablished Olympic Games in 1896. Then, possibly inspired by pools recently discovered in colonial India, swimming pools began to be built in England, and their use spread to Europe,

Australia, and America.

In Australia, the first seawater pool was built near Brisbane in 1819. Due to its popularity, and encouraged by a warm, Mediterranean-style climate, pools extended along Australia's east coast over the next hundred years.

One of the first public pools in the United States was built in Brookline, Massachusetts, in 1887. Soon other cities followed suit, especially in California. Pools quickly became the province of the rich and famous. Mary Pickford and Douglas Fairbanks built a pool in 1920 at their Pickfair mansion in Beverly Hills that was large enough to float a canoe, while compulsive builder William Randolph Hearst installed a swimming pool at his palatial California showplace,

San Simeon, in 1924, that he later reworked into the Neptune Pool, surrounded by marble colonnades.

By the 1920s, American architects began to integrate swimming pools into their house plans. Richard Neutra's Lovell Health House, with its innovative sprayed-concrete pool, was built in 1929, while Frank Lloyd Wright added one to his 1924 Ennis House in 1940, using the same concrete blocks as he had in the iconic Aztec-like main building.

This new enthusiasm for swimming pools was ignited by the legendary swimmer Esther Williams, who popularized swimming as an everyday sport in the 1940s. Called "America's mermaid," she swam through many movies in revealing bathing suits, introducing aquatics for the first time to an enthusiastic audience. By the 1970s, there were more than a million pools in the United States, mostly in suburban backyards. This was a big step as the swimming pool was no longer just in the realm of Hollywood and the very rich. Helped by cheaper construction materials, servicemen returning from World War II found themselves buying brand-new suburban tract houses, which often came complete with swimming pools and the accompanying lifestyle. With

OPPOSITE, TOP LEFT: Sydney's Bondi Icebergs Club ocean pool was built out of coastal rock in 1929. OPPOSITE, TOP RIGHT: Artist Ed Ruscha created an artwork for the bottom of a swimming pool belonging to his brother, Paul Ruscha. ABOVE, LEFT: Mary Pickford and Douglas Fairbanks at Pickfair, their home in Beverly Hills. ABOVE, RIGHT: Frank Lloyd Wright's Ennis House had an "early" private pool, added in 1940.

LEFT: The Yucatán Peninsula has many water holes, called cenotes. Once used for ceremonies, they have now become public water holes and popular places to dive. **OPPOSITE**: Artist and designer Dana Westring overcame the disadvantages of a sloping ground when he installed his pool in Virginia.

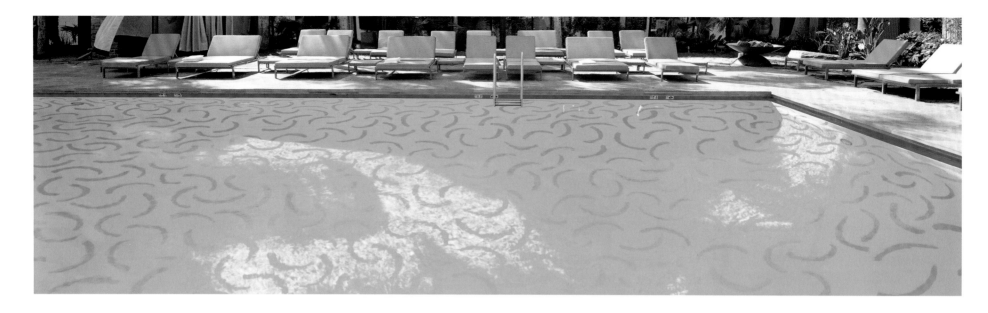

the development of heaters, underwater lighting, auto-fill sensors, and valves, pool construction was made even easier in the 1950s and 1960s.

It was only a matter of time before these ubiquitous symbols of suburbia came to the attention of artists and photographers. Californian artist Ed Ruscha responded in 1968 with an artist's book titled *Nine Swimming Pools and a Broken Glass*, photographed in Las Vegas. Later on he created the artwork for a pool in the San Fernando Valley for his brother, the photographer Paul Ruscha. However, one of the most famous painters of swimming pools is David Hockney, whose painting *A Bigger Splash* of 1967 came to define a particular moment in time in Beverly Hills. He went on to paint the inside of his own pool around 1978, as well as a large one commissioned for the Hollywood Roosevelt hotel in 1988. The East Coast painter

Eric Fischl brings a more unnerving perspective to the ubiquity of the suburban swimming pool, using them in his realistic paintings as backdrops of disconnection in family relationships.

Despite countless appearances in art, film, and literature, a swimming pool does more than function as a stage for human drama. It can enhance life dramatically, as thousands of Americans discovered after World War II. To be able to create a private oasis at home was a completely new invention; this pursuit began a new wave of design incorporating water, plants, and architecture, which we hope to continue to inspire and encourage with this book.

ABOVE: Artist David Hockney was commissioned to add artwork to the Hollywood Roosevelt hotel swimming pool in 1988. OPPOSITE: David Hockney painted his own pool in the Hollywood Hills around 1978, which served as the inspiration for the Hollywood Roosevelt's pool nearly ten years later.

GARDEN POOLS

Landscaping Oases

There is nothing more beautiful than a perfectly proportioned swimming pool, especially when it can double as an ornamental pond. Either designed for an urban backyard or spread out in the comparatively unlimited spaces of a country property, a pool immediately transforms any home into a luxury resort. In the suburbs, a well-planned garden can transform a swimming pool from a clear-cut, hard-edged rectangle in the middle of a backyard to a verdant oasis. This is not always easy as plants and trees have to be chosen carefully to act as a screen, being mindful of dropped leaves, which need a lot of cleaning up—as picturesque as a pond full of blossoms may look, pool maintenance becomes a constant job of fishing out the leaves, berries, and plant pods.

Getting the planting right is very rewarding, as Simon Doonan and Jonathan Adler discovered when the addition of cold-climate, no-fuss bamboo gave their Shelter Island pool a California vibe in the Hamptons. Like many pools today, theirs is a fashionable dark blue, darker than the swimming pools from the 1960s, which were usually a vivid aqua color.

Today, a beachside pool in a garden setting is designed to spill open to the elements of sun and sea, so pool colors are often brighter. The color is determined by the choice of paint or concrete dye for the pool lining. To achieve blue water, the finish should be white, blue, or gray. For a green, more natural color, the pigment would be a light brown or green. Interestingly enough, dark pools are estimated to stay about five degrees cooler than pools of a lighter color.

When planning the landscaping of a pool, the first step is to find the largest available perimeter, usually the lot boundary, and begin there with trees or large shrubs for security, shade, and privacy. The plantings provide a vertical element to the landscape. Then lower-growing plants, chosen according to the climate, can be brought into grow closer to the pool. They may include a low hedge, or perhaps a row of dwarf palms, that can also define a small lawn or deck. Some very successful pools have plants right up to the coping, which softens its hard edge. A big swathe of unused decking surrounding the pool can make it look too inhospitable, so the coping should either extend from the pool to form a deck for outdoor chairs and tables, or be a thin stone border that separates a lawn from the water. For a more natural effect, the edge can even be covered by wood decking. Some gardens have greenery growing up to one side of the pool or over a nearby high wall. You will find there are many planting options, which vary according to climate and spatial opportunities.

OPPOSITE: Inspired by old *Sunset* magazines, Simon Doonan and Jonathan Adler added a swimming pool to the backyard of their former house on Shelter Island. Weather-resistant bamboo gives the garden a California vibe.

It can be easy to create a graceful oasis that sits harmoniously in the garden. Even in harsh climates large plants in ornamental pots can add landscaping to the pool with little effort; they can be brought indoors during the winter. In summer, author Carolyne Roehm surrounds her Connecticut swimming pool with topiary-filled blue-and-white ceramic pots, giving it the look of an ornamental pond.

Local fencing laws are one of the biggest design challenges architects and landscapers face. How do you secure the area but prevent the pool area from resembling a maximum-security stockade surrounded by harsh railings or chain-link fencing? Each city or town has its own code, but generally the surrounding fence should be at least four feet high and have a gate with a childproof latch. A lot of creative effort goes into disguising the fencing while retaining the style of the house. These include sandwiching a chain-link fence between two rows of evergreen hedges, while making a feature of the entry gate, adding encircling rock walls, or even surrounding the pool with a transparent fence.

Well-designed patios and pool houses for parties and meals add to the enjoyment of the area and are often included in the master plan. Pool houses add enormously to the appreciation of a pool, providing shade as well as a comfortable place to relax. They can include indoor kitchens or shelter outdoor appliances, and house many other amenities, as well as a convenient place to watch children at play. They can provide washing machines for bathing suits and towels or serve as a space for meditation, a gym, or overnight houseguests. Designer Suzanne Rheinstein reworked a garage at one end of her Los Angeles swimming pool so she could hold large dinner parties in front of a fireplace while overlooking the pool.

In Hawaii, Doris Duke's oriental-themed guesthouse at Shangri La includes an unfurnished long, shady loggia at one end of her pool, while the pavilion designed by Martyn Lawrence Bullard for his client Chris Cortazzo in Malibu is filled with comfortable indoor/outdoor armchairs and a flat-screen TV. Not everyone has room for a pool house or gazebo—a roof overhang or shady vine-filled trellis, arbor, or pergola can provide shade instead.

Lap pools were first seen in California in the 1970s. They were specifically designed for exercise as their long, narrow shape made it easy for a swimmer to swim up and down doing laps. These pools also conveniently fitted into narrow backyards, and became ideal for small gardens. Usually landscaped like larger pools, they sometimes have raised edging that serves as seating. Architect Manolo Mestre built one in his own

OPPOSITE: Carolyne Roehm's pool at Weatherstone, her Litchfield County home, is lined with elegant blue-and-white china plant pots in summer.

OPPOSITE: Decorator Suzanne Rheinstein converted a garage into a pool house for entertaining at her home in Los Angeles.

RIGHT: The back of designer and author Florence de Dampierre's Colonial Revival house in Litchfield, Connecticut, has a sweeping view of the swimming pool and garden.

PAGE 22: This variation on a traditional rectangular pool shape allows for extra landscaping. It was designed by Mario Nievera for a house in Palm Beach, Florida.

PAGE 23: New York architects Smith-Miller + Hawkinson designed this Los Angeles pool on a separate lot to take advantage of the view.

OPPOSITE: Designer Bunny Williams's rustic pool-house temple above her Connecticut house was inspired by local Falls Village Greek Revival architecture.
RIGHT: Architect Manolo Mestre designed a long lap pool to fit his garden in Mérida, Mexico.
PAGE 26: Robert Evans's Hollywood Regency pool and pavilion, designed by John Elgin Woolf, is edged by a circular row of fountains.
PAGE 27: Decorator and author Hutton Wilkinson designed and furnished this pool to double as an ornamental pond. He added the steps up to an outdoor dining terrace.

long, slim garden in Mérida, Mexico, and added an underwater bench so that friends could sit along one side of the pool.

It is interesting to note that, as a decorative element in the garden, rectangular pools are today's most popular shape, while the kidney-shaped pool favored in the 1950s and 1960s has become almost obsolete.

In the country, a swimming pool can transform the landscape. It can give purpose to the garden, which becomes an elegant architectural gesture, as well as a retreat from the rest of the property. This type of pool can add drama to the look of a house, expanding the layout of the property by becoming a destination point, especially if placed at some distance from the house. In Connecticut, decorator Bunny Williams placed her rustic templelike pool house and stone-edged pool at a distant angle to the main house, creating its own territory with a separate view. A path curves around an open field back to her barn. It draws people into her much-published large garden, which is often open to the public.

LEFT: Jewelry designer Liv Ballard commissioned pool furniture from the author for her Beverly Hills pool, which is screened by a planting of tall hedges and palm trees. OPPOSITE: Hutton Wilkinson's swimming pool at Dawnridge, the Tony Duquette estate in Beverly Hills, is enlivened by bright red Chinese root-wood chairs. PAGE 30: Coordinated pool furniture, added by designer Tom Beeton, defines a small pool in California. PAGE 31: Architect Steven Ehrlich designed this Californian pool, which is screened by a row of bamboo plantings.

OPPOSITE: Antiquarian and designer Richard Shapiro is also an accomplished landscapist. He planned his Californian garden to resemble his favorite gardens in Italy. RIGHT: Shapiro built a pool house with the perfect proportions of a Palladian villa at the other end of the swimming pool. PAGE 34: Collector Barry Sloane reworked his pool at the Le Château de Cardet to line up with his guesthouse, a former farm building with classical Palladian proportions. PAGE 35: A classically landscaped pool in Montecito, California, is flanked by cypress trees.

LEFT: Jim Watterson and George Martin added a small pool to the back garden courtyard of Casa Capricho, their house in San Miguel de Allende, Mexico. **OPPOSITE**: A well-designed courtyard pool, which includes a statue of San Miguel in the wall niche, at Casa Tortuga in San Miguel de Allende.

LEFT: New York decorator Juan Montoya based the design of his swimming pool on a floor pattern from a Swedish palace. BELOW: At the Villa Bebek in Bali, tropical landscape designer and author Made Wijaya designed and landscaped his verdant garden, including a swimming pool detail inspired by David Hockney. OPPOSITE: Hotel and resort designer Alexandra Champalimaud added a decorative flourish to her Connecticut pool.

LEFT: The pool at the Abernathy House in Palm Springs, California, includes a fire pit at one end. A marble elephant is a fixed part of the pool's decor. BELOW: Decorator Martyn Lawrence Bullard redesigned this Palm Springs pool expressly for entertaining. He added an outdoor bar in the garden, as well as a bar pit and in-pool stools for swim-up cocktails. OPPOSITE: Gray Organschi Architecture designed Simon Doonan and Jonathan Adler's new house on Shelter Island, including a pool house, which was planned to have views of both the pool and the ocean.

LEFT: Michael Booth of the San Francisco firm BAMO designed this circular pool next to a natural lake for the McEvoy olive ranch in Marin County. OPPOSITE: Martyn Lawrence Bullard decorated this pool with views across the Pacific Ocean at Casa Aramara in Punta Mita, Mexico, for an American client. PAGE 44: Fabric designer Sharyn Storrier Lyneham and her husband, Dr. Robert Lyneham, reworked their pool in Sydney, Australia, to upgrade the landscaping as well as its shape. The transparent fence helped the pool conform to local building codes. PAGE 45: 1stdibs founder Michael Bruno landscaped his Southampton beach house pool area to include a sheltered outdoor table for meals.

LEFT: Gusky Suarsana brought in designer Made Wijaya to add a swimming pool to his family property in Bali. A row of traditional-style Balinese fountains was installed on one side of the pool. BELOW: Decorator Martyn Lawrence Bullard edged a pool in the hills above Malibu with ornamental pots for Realtor Chris Cortazzo. OPPOSITE: Garden designer Nancy Goslee Power included low-water plantings as well as a rose garden for a Brentwood, California, property.

OPPOSITE: The swimming pool at the Hollister House Garden in Connecticut has been designed by owner George Schoellkopf to resemble an ornamental pond. Partially owned by the Garden Conservancy, this property is open to the public in summer. RIGHT: Designer Made Wijaya landscaped his pool at the Villa Bebek in Bali to include tropical plantings right up to the edge of the water. PAGE 50: Paul Fortune decorated this Beverly Hills house, which includes a tiled fountain centrally placed in front of the swimming pool. PAGE 51: The distinguished Los Angeles landscaper Nancy Goslee Power designed this garden in California's Pacific Palisades.

OPPOSITE: Architects Tichenor & Thorp in Los Angeles designed this garden for a previous director of the J. Paul Getty Museum with a blue-and-white tiled trim. RIGHT: Californian landscape designer Nancy Goslee Power created this small ornamental pool as a central focus for her courtyard. PAGE 54: Martyn Lawrence Bullard furnished this Beverly Hills pool with "trim green" Sunbrella fabrics. A gazebo covered in flowering vines provides shade. PAGE 55: This central courtyard swimming pool is inside a classic John Elgin Woolf Regency Revival building, occupied by a clothing store called the Row.

LEFT: Plain wood decking forms a practical terrace around this hillside pool in Bali. OPPOSITE: The pool house at Casa Arcadia in Mexico's Cuixmala resort was designed by Duccio Ermenegildo. The curved lines of the pool follow the natural contours of the site. PAGE 58: The large pool at the Hacienda de San Antonio in Mexico was designed by Robert Couturier in the resort's beautifully landscaped gardens. PAGE 59: The pool at the Leff-Florsheim House, designed by Donald Wexler in Palm Springs, California, has stepped terraces leading down from the house, which includes a raised Jacuzzi.

LEFT: Suzanne McKevitt designed this clever step-down pool and entertainment area in Los Angeles. BELOW: KAA Design introduced abstract transitional lawn spaces leading to this generous-sized Californian pool. OPPOSITE: Architect Steven Ehrlich designed this Californian pool in a sloping garden, shadowed by native sycamore trees. PAGE 62: Considered one of his best works, landscape designer Lockwood de Forest III created the gardens at Val Verde in Montecito, California. The architect of this private villa, built in the 1920s, was Bertram Goodhue. PAGE 63: The singer Cher's house in Malibu has a pool that reaches out to the Pacific Ocean. Her decorator, Martyn Lawrence Bullard, added the contemplative statue at one end.

LEFT: The pool at the Hacienda Petac was created from an old irrigation tank in the Yucatán, Mexico. The designers Reyes Rios + Larrain added a gazebo to provide shade. OPPOSITE: The lap pool at La Meta, in Mexico, was designed by artist Mari Carmen Hernandez with help from her architect friend Duccio Ermenegildo. PAGE 66: The pool on a sloping Montecito hillside was planned to include a series of terraces and decorative retaining walls as part of the design of the garden. PAGE 67: Collector and Realtor Barry Sloane designed the stonework around a pool to match his eighteenth-century château outbuildings in France. He carefully modulated the muted blue color of the swimming pool to appear less artificial.

LEFT: An elegantly designed pool and deck in Montauk. BELOW: Every cottage at the hotel Puri Ganesha in Bali has its own pool, which looks out to the ocean past a landscaped garden. OPPOSITE: Decorator Thomas Hamel created the pool terrace overlooking Sydney Harbor, which can be seen through the clear safety fence.

LEFT: Artist Jorge Pardo designed this long lap pool in his narrow Mérida courtyard. OPPOSITE: Decorator Steven Gambrel added a pool and a pavilion to this Sag Harbor garden. PAGE 72: A swimming pool in the entry courtyard of Casa Palikao, in San Miguel de Allende, Mexico. PAGE 73: This terrace pool has high-level views of San Miguel de Allende, Mexico.

LEFT: At Shangri La, the Doris Duke estate in Hawaii, a stepped garden leads from the pool to the main house.
OPPOSITE: The dramatic guesthouse at the other end of the pool was designed by the principal project architect Marion Sims Wyeth in the late 1930s.

ARCHITECTURAL POOLS
Integrated Swimming Pools

One of the most compelling reasons to hire an architect rather than just a contractor when building a new house is to include an integrated swimming pool in the design plan. With the help of a professional, the pool can be designed to relate to the living space, enhancing both the building and the pool at the same time. Skillful design and placement can transform even an ordinary suburban lot into a significant architectural accomplishment. A Los Angeles house by Steven Ehrlich for his family has a lap pool right up against the front of the small lot that is overshadowed by the building. By using the roof to suspend colorful canvas shades and designing sliding doors, which open almost directly onto the pool, the architect added significant drama to what would otherwise be an undistinguished narrow garden space.

When there is more space, such as in a large urban garden or in the country, a swimming pool can be designed as a destination point, reached by paths that form an architectural framework for the space. A pool can become part of the view or add to it, especially if it resembles a pond or natural body of water.

Architectural detailing can be synchronized so that the pool either becomes part of the house, or acts as a continuation of the shape of the building. When it is part of the

physical structure of the house, a pool becomes a negotiation between interior and exterior living spaces. Bringing water into the building adds an extra interior design element. It can be considered a "room in the house filled with water," which adds a dramatic element that also helps cool the inside and reflect light, especially in tropical climates where buildings are often purposely left open to the elements.

An indoor pool can either be in an enclosed room, like the Brody House, designed by A. Quincy Jones, and once owned by actress Ellen DeGeneres, or flow through the house in unexpected ways. In the Elrod House in Palm Springs, designed by architect John Lautner, the shape of the indoor-outdoor pool echoes the architectural detailing of the roof. Glass doors slide over the pool to separate it from the outdoors in the cool desert evenings.

Pritzker prize-winning Mexican architect Luis Barragán designed the indoor pool inside his iconic Gilardi House in vivid primary colors, which are used throughout the house. Years later, the architect Ricardo Legoretta, inspired by Barragán, also used bright colors when he designed the Casa Colorada pool in Valle de Bravo, opening the indoor pool area, with its bright pink walls, to the outdoors using large, open-glass windows.

A swimming pool placed directly next to the house in the landscape can act as a reflecting element, or a moat. It

OPPOSITE: The indoor pool echoes the architecture in this futuristic house in Palm Springs, California, designed by architect John Lautner.

also becomes part of the architecture of the house if similar materials or shapes are used. This kind of pool can be an extension of the building, acting as an extra "room," especially if the kitchen opens directly onto it, which makes it handy for entertaining. If a pool is used primarily for exercising, it can be planned to lead from the bedroom or gym.

Another advantage of building from scratch means using the same stone or building material throughout—from the garden walls at the front of the house, through the house, and then around the pool as well as continuing to the rear wall of the property. This provides a harmonious transition throughout the whole project.

In the Sassoon House, by Los Angeles architect Hal Levitt, the swimming pool flows under a glassed-in walkway, continuing into a small landscaped exterior courtyard. When the sliding glass doors are opened, the relationship of the pool to the house becomes dramatically sculptural. In Frank Gehry's Schnabel House, a long lap pool appears to float along the side of the buildings, becoming an added architectural element to the collection of pavilions that form the property. Water can also reflect light back into the building, such as in the Singleton House, by Richard Neutra, or mirror the building itself, like the Napa Valley swimming pool designed by architect David Connor, which reflects its tall, elegant pool tower.

Architects can create shade by extending the building to shelter one end, or even the entire pool. This can be as simple as a skeleton structure to support canvas, or a more complex solution involving an upper floor. In a house in tropical Bali for photographer Jan Tyniec and fashion designer Christyne Forti, architect Cheong Yew Kuan extended a triangular section of the roof off one end of the house. Here, the scenic valley below is seen from the sheltered pool, which acts as a watery viewing deck.

In a windy climate, the house can wrap around the pool to protect it, or enclose an inner courtyard, like the Lloyd Wright–designed Samuel-Novarro House in Los Feliz, restored by actress Diane Keaton. In the small Richard Neutra–designed Miller House in Palm Springs, the pool fits neatly roofed inside an exterior alcove.

If space is limited, architects can design a house to hold a pool on the roof, where it becomes a platform for upper-level views. At the Standard hotel in downtown Los Angeles, the architects Koning Eizenberg sited a large pool a dizzyingly twelve stories above the busy urban streets. One could also be built on top of a house in any urban area, especially where there are scenic views of an attractive park or nearby mountains. Whether starting with an empty lot, or in an unbuilt landscape, here we show that bringing in an architect produces a beautifully integrated pool.

PAGE 78: Designer Jane Hallworth worked with Ellen DeGeneres and Portia de Rossi to renovate their A. Quincy Jones house in Los Angeles, which included this indoor spa. PAGE 79: In Bali, architect Cheong Yew Kuan designed a house and pool for Jan Tyniec and Christyne Forti to maximize the views over a beautiful tropical valley. RIGHT: This Los Angeles house, designed by Steven Ehrlich for his family, has a lap pool located right up against the front of the small lot. Using colorful blinds to screen the pool, the architect has added drama to an undistinguished narrow, garden space.

LEFT: Richard Neutra's Singleton House incorporates a small pool of water to visually extend the indoor space.

OPPOSITE: The swimming pool designed by architect Hal Levitt flows under a bridge, which connects two parts of his house. The sliding glass windows can be pulled back to create an open space.

OPPOSITE: In Bali, architect Cheong Yew Kuan planned this pool as an abstract shape to reflect the structure of the house he built for Jan Tyniec and Christyne Forti. RIGHT: The Schnabel House was designed by Frank Gehry as several individual structures. He included the long lap pool as an additional architectural embellishment. PAGE 86: Cedric Gibbons created a house for his then-wife, actress Dolores Del Río, in 1930. It included a swimming pool, which was then a rare luxury. PAGE 87: The Davis House in Palm Springs was designed by Henry Eggers and Walter Wilkman in 1957. The pool is surrounded by a colonnaded loggia on three sides.

LEFT: Architect David Connor planned this pool in Napa Valley to connect the main house and a tower-like study, which is reflected in the water. OPPOSITE: The Standard hotel's rooftop pool was built by Los Angeles architects Koning Eizenberg as part of an adaptive reuse of the historic Superior Oil building in 2002, showing the merits of a rooftop pool when there is no available garden space. PAGE 90: Architect Hal Levitt visually floated the pool into his Beverly Hills house, creating an extra architectural element to the proportions of the building. PAGE 91: Designer Martyn Lawrence Bullard reconfigured his Alexander House pool in Palm Springs to span the length of the front of the main building.

LEFT: Architect Glen Irani took advantage of the built-in shaded area when he located the pool under the house he designed in Venice, California. OPPOSITE: Zoltan Pali created a built-in deck, which leads to the corner of the pool closest to back of the house. PAGE 94: In 1976, Luis Barragán designed the indoor pool of the Gilardi House in Mexico City, adding bold strokes of color. This was the Pritzker prize-winning architect's final commission. PAGE 95: Architect Ricardo Legorreta included this indoor pool in a house in Valle de Bravo, Mexico. He used vivid color to frame the views through the large window-like openings. PAGES 96 AND 97: Mexican architect Luis Barragán designed these iconic stables in 1968, and included a large exercise pool for the horses. A fountain spills water into the pool.

LEFT: Frank Lloyd Wright's son, Lloyd Wright, designed the Samuel-Novarro House, which includes a pool courtyard, in 1928. It was later restored by actress Diane Keaton. OPPOSITE: In Mérida, architect Chip Bohl reworked the back of a house owned by David Serrano and Robert Willson, and added a swimming pool. He created a broad deck on one side for entertaining. PAGE 100: Architect Arcadio Marín built a studio, called Plantel Matilde, in the Yucatán Peninsula for his brother, Javier. He placed an architecturally elegant swimming pool within the building's colonnades. PAGE 101: Designer Martyn Lawrence Bullard's own house in Palm Springs, by architect James McNaughton, features his tile designs for Ann Sacks. His indoor-outdoor furniture surrounds the spa area at the end of the pool.

LEFT: Richard Neutra's 1959 Singleton House in Los Angeles has a moat-like pool, which reflects light back into the house. OPPOSITE: The view of the Singleton swimming pool is linked to the reflecting pool. PAGE 104: The 1967 Cody Glass House pool has a dramatic view of the San Jacinto Mountains above Palm Springs. PAGE 105: Richard Neutra's Kaufmann House is one of Palm Springs' most iconic residences. The pool is centered in the garden with views of the house.

OPPOSITE: Frank Lloyd Wright's last project was the Norman Lykes House in Arizona. The pool wall echoes the circular theme of the house.
RIGHT: The Sheats-Goldstein House by architect John Lautner shelters the pool with its coffered concrete living room roof.

LEFT: The Beyer residence by John Lautner in Malibu includes a concrete wave-like roof over the swimming pool. BELOW: The swimming pool at a beach house, designed by architect John Lautner in Malibu, is cleverly folded into the wings of the building. OPPOSITE: Architect Steven Ehrlich designed a sliding panel at the end of the pool to open the garden, landscaped by Barry Beer, to the Santa Monica beach. PAGE 110: The Singleton House swimming pool was designed by Richard Neutra to complement the modernist architecture of the main house. PAGE 111: John Lautner designed what was perhaps the first infinity edge pool for Silvertop, a house he built in 1957 in Silver Lake, a Los Angeles neighborhood.

OPPOSITE: The iconic Stahl House has one of the most celebrated modern pools in Los Angeles. Designed by architect Pierre Koenig in 1960, it is known as Case Study House 22.
RIGHT: Architect Mark Rios reworked this house by Lloyd Wright, the son of Frank Lloyd Wright, to include an infinity pool at the rear of the lot to take advantage of its hillside setting.

LEFT: Designed for actor Gary Cooper by architect A. Quincy Jones in the 1950s, this dramatically modern house includes an open gazebo facing the pool. OPPOSITE: Brazilian architect Oscar Neimeyer only had one project in the United States—the Strick House. The pool he designed overlooks Santa Monica canyon. FOLLOWING SPREAD: John Lautner's Harpel House, built in 1956, was recently restored by homeowner and designer Mark Haddawy. Lautner enjoyed creating pools with dramatic views over Los Angeles.

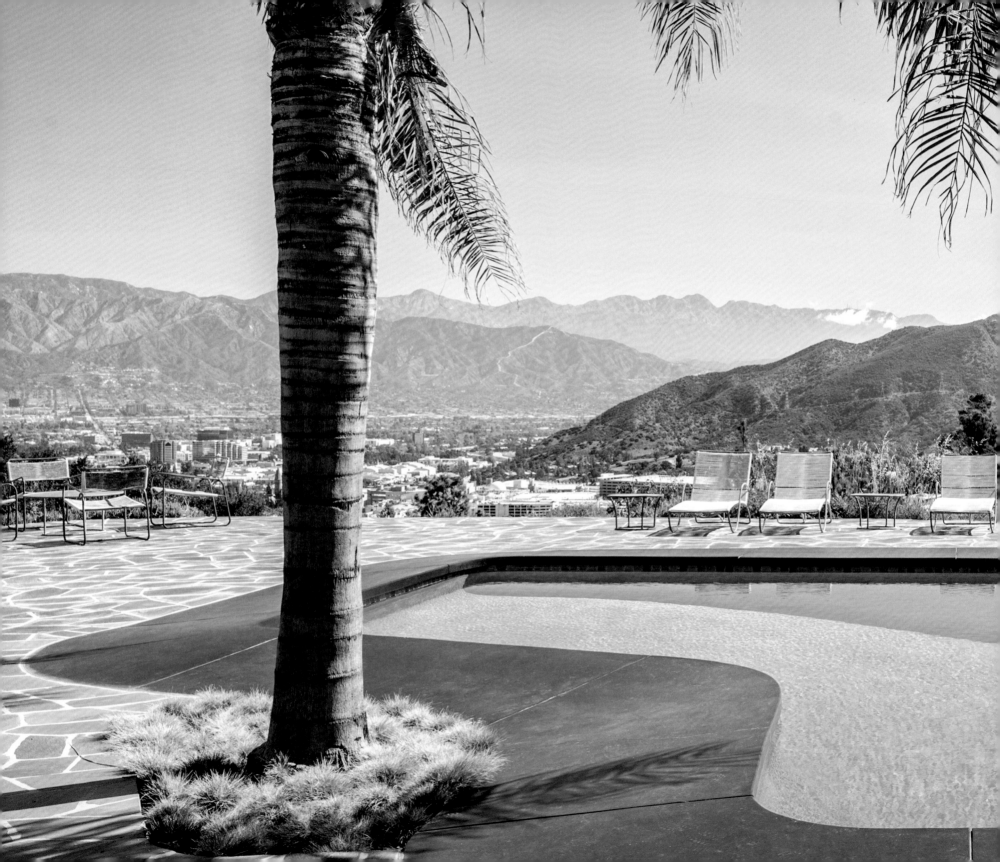

INFINITY POOLS

The Vanishing Edge

There are several theories about who invented the infinity pool. A classic resort staple, especially by the ocean, where its edge is designed to merge with the watery horizon, this kind of pool has a visual effect that gives the bather a sense of infinity, hence its name. Most likely it was architect John Lautner, whose house, Silvertop, built in 1957 on a Los Angeles hill overlooking the shimmering Silver Lake Reservoir, included the first infinity pool.

These are the most dramatic of swimming pools, usually situated on a slope to highlight the view, but structurally, they can be difficult to build. They are created by lowering one (or sometimes both) lengths of the sides of the pool rim to just below the water surface, creating a spill of water out of the pool and into a receiving trench below, which circulates it back into the pool.

Infinity pools are usually architecturally very pure in their design, and their location is often carefully chosen due to their complex construction methods. They are usually found wherever there is an amazing view of city lights or a dramatic landscape often overlooking the ocean, and can be designed to appear to merge with their surroundings. Distant mountains reflect in the still water, and a rocky edge can merge into the landscape.

When creating an infinity pool, the style of the accompanying house is always important. However, these pools

OPPOSITE: Realtor and collector Barry Sloane designed his Los Feliz pool to have two infinity edges. ABOVE: Infinity pools can add drama when positioned to take in the view of the surrounding countryside. Here, architect Ricardo Legorreta designed a pool overlooking California's Napa Valley.

look just as good beside a modernist house in Palm Springs as next to a thatched-roof retreat in Mexico or Bali. But the extra structural expense of installing an infinity pool might not make it a worthwhile choice for an ordinary suburban back lot, especially as every pool is custom made.

Realtor and collector Barry Sloane has designed one of the tallest infinity pools in Los Angeles. Built with a twenty-six-foot drop, he has gone to a lot of trouble to avoid the problem of efflorescence, a salt-based stain on the supporting structure caused when water spills down its side. Here, he used a supporting wall of uneven marble chips with a Franco-Italian inspired design to avoid the appearance of streaks.

To swim up to the view is one of the great pleasures of an infinity pool, so they are often rectangular in shape. These pools are as ideal for peaceful contemplation as exercise. To be in water right at the edge of a cliff or a tropical valley is a sensational experience. Landscape designer and author Made Wijaya added a small pool to serve several of his guesthouses near Ubud in Bali. With its infinity edge overlooking one of the most beautiful terraced valleys on the island, it becomes much more than a typical tropical retreat.

Beach houses in the small resort town of Careyes have some of the most elegant swimming pools in Mexico. Perched along a steep cliff, with difficult access down to the beach, this is a perfect location for an infinity pool designed to blend into the sea and blue sky and colored to closely match the water below. Here, at Casa Luna, architect Manolo Mestre created a pool that follows the curve of the cliff, providing a watery barrier between the house and the ocean below.

A dramatic house in Nichols Canyon, high above Los Angeles, has a spectacular infinity pool designed by XTEN Architecture with Kravitz Design, which overlooks a 180-degree view of the city. Here we see the full theatrical potential of these types of pools, as not only does it have lighted steps leading out toward the view, but it also manages to contain a fire pit inside a large rock placed several feet from the edge in the water. Next to it bubbles a small fountain.

The enthusiasm for infinity pools has coincided with the evolution of the hotel as a spa retreat, and this has filtered through to the lifestyle at home. Many people return home wanting to replicate their resort experience, and building an infinity pool is an important part of continuing the fantasy.

OPPOSITE: Landscape designer Made Wijaya added a contour to the edge of his infinity pool at the Taman Bebek in Bali, giving it a more organic shape. PAGE 122: A beautiful infinity pool, designed by Duccio Ermenegildo, on a cliff in Careyes, Mexico. PAGE 123: Overlooking Los Angeles, this glamorous pool, designed by XTEN Architecture with Kravitz Design, features a fire pit.

OPPOSITE: Isabel Goldsmith's infinity pool near Las Alamandas, her resort hotel in Mexico, was designed by architect Manolo Mestre and blends in seamlessly with the ocean beyond. RIGHT: Broad steps lead down to fashion designer Tommy Hilfiger's pool built directly in the sand in Mustique.

LEFT: An edge detail of Made Wijaya's infinity pool at the Taman Bebek in Bali shows the use of pebbles as a surface material. OPPOSITE: Architect Manolo Mestre designed a vacation house in Careyes, Mexico, for his client Chris Tribull, with soft curved contours and a "beach."

LEFT: The unusual urban double-edge infinity pool in Los Feliz was designed by Barry Sloane. BELOW: The spa attached to the Sloane House pool was created to make the most of a striking view over Los Angeles. OPPOSITE: Stretching dramatically out into the view in Bali, this pool at the Villa Kelusa makes the most of its rustic, tropical surroundings. The property was decorated by Lloyd Hassencahl of Design Solutions.

PAGE 130: The author contemplates the sea in a small infinity pool at the Four Seasons Resort at Jimbaran Bay, Bali. With landscaping by Made Wijaya, each villa pool has a view of the ocean. PAGE 131: An infinity pool in Careyes, Mexico, connects visually with a distant ocean view. OPPOSITE: This small infinity pool by Diego Villaseñor takes full advantage of the lakeside view at the Mexican resort Valle de Bravo. RIGHT: Landscape designer Made Wijaya created this elegantly minimal infinity pool in Bali.

OPPOSITE: Designer Giorgio Brignoni's infinity pool looks over a tropical landscape in Mexico.
RIGHT: This Strawberry Hill infinity pool offers a view over Kingston, Jamaica. The resort is part of a chain of hotels owned by Chris Blackwell.

LEFT: Landscape designer Jay Griffith added a soft bamboo planting around a pool by architect Steven Ehrlich in Los Angeles. RIGHT: This sublimely elegant infinity pool in Careyes, Mexico, was designed by Gian Franco Brignone. PAGE 138: Architect Cheong Yew Kuan chose to set this high-level streamlined pool back from a cliff overlooking the ocean in Bali. PAGE 139: Isabel Goldsmith built this small pool for one of the larger casitas at her resort hotel, Las Alamandas, in Mexico.

LEFT: In the Dominican Republic, Duccio Ermenegildo designed this unusual elliptical infinity pool to sit flat in the beachside garden.
OPPOSITE: Ermenegildo designed this pool at Casa Torre to look out across the ecological Cuixmala resort, near Careyes, Mexico.

RIGHT: Duccio Ermenegildo designed this infinity pool to mimic the contours of the nearby cliff with a sinuous S-curve.

FANTASY POOLS

Creating Dreams

The best thing about fantasy pools is that there are no rules, only safety concerns that should be realistically navigated. These are perhaps the most wonderful swimming pools as they are designed to fuel the imagination and to create a splendid illusion.

When swimming pools first became popular in the twentieth century, designers naturally looked to the past for inspiration. Conventional fountains have been widespread in Asia and Europe since at least the sixth century BCE. In ancient Greece and Rome, it was fashionable to create water fantasies in the garden—all kinds of grottos, rills, and ponds often festooned with sculptures. But it wasn't until the sixteenth century that fountains became established garden devices in the rest of Europe. During the eighteenth century, the British were keen builders of purely decorative garden buildings, called follies, where they enthusiastically reproduced Roman temples, Egyptian pyramids, and Chinese pagodas for their country estates.

We can see this influence in fantasy gardens today. Greek columns, rock waterfalls, thatched cottages, ruinscapes, and elaborate fountains are some of the many designs used in these kinds of pools, both private and public, which are planned to specifically create a fantasy world. Transforming a suburban garden into a personal and poetic vision of exotic rock pools and tropical lagoons can be an exciting project. Much like creating a magical stage set, an imaginative pool can become a world within a world and serve as a retreat from daily life as a wonderful, watery experience.

While there are no real rules for fantasy pools, there are several types. One would be an elaborate design inside the pool, such as in the Paley House pool, part of an estate designed by the architect Paul Williams in the 1930s. This extraordinarily detailed mosaic representing the twelve signs of the zodiac was designed to complement the main house by landscapist Edward Huntsman-Trout.

Another strategy is to create a fantasy surrounding the pool itself. For example, one could include a circular pool house in the middle of a round swimming pool, as seen in Palm Springs, or surround a more conventional rectangular-shaped pool with Greek columns built out of recycled street lamps—all these are marvelous and inspirational ideas.

Decorator and artist Tony Duquette created an exotic pool at Dawnridge, his Beverly Hills estate, where he designed two tall shell-covered obelisks to define its garden entry. His

OPPOSITE: The style of the 1962 George Randolph Hearst pool in Palm Springs was influenced by the Neptune Pool at his father's legendary estate, San Simeon, and even includes statues gifted from San Simeon.

swimming pool overlooks a small valley, which Duquette filled with stepped oriental pagodas and an ornamental pond. This was a spectacular gesture, quite unexpected in suburban Beverly Hills. In Miami, the late designer Gianni Versace constructed a mosaic templelike architectural wall complete with urns and arches as a fantasy backdrop to his pool, while the Neptune Pool in the Hearst Castle is overlooked by a life-size granite and marble Greco-Roman temple.

Sometimes the fantasy is supplied almost entirely by the pool's location. The Hart pool, near Ubud in Bali, is a simple free-form infinity pool that sits like a watery rice field on the edge of one of the most exotic corners of the world, overlooking a spectacular tropical valley. The setting can also be part of the fantasy—a view of distant mountains enhancing a boulder-strewn pool, or a plantation of palm trees as an exotic backdrop. A pool suspended over an ocean view provides a very different experience, as infinity pools blur the line between the pool and the ocean. These include the element of fantasy, as they can be perched dramatically on a hillside, or even on top of a skyscraper. The swimming pools at the Amankila hotel in Bali are world famous, as they step down the slope with a magnificent view of the ocean beyond.

Gazebos filled with cushions furnish each end of the three pools. Usually such elaborate infinity pools are part of a resort hotel, although they can be included in private gardens, preferably with a view.

Occasionally, these pools may be designed to have sandy beaches at one end, where water slopes gently away from a hidden edge, or they are built with central islands and gazebos reached by a bridge or two. Swimming through rooms of an open, ancient building in a pool at the Hacienda Puerta Campeche, on Mexico's Yucatán Peninsula, is a surreal experience. When the architects restored its dilapidated nineteenth-century buildings, they kept several adjoining structures open to the elements, and flowed a swimming pool through several of the rooms. This fantasy pool gives bathers the unexpected experience of exploring the property by swimming through it, or they can simply enjoy the space from one of the hammocks suspended across the water.

OPPOSITE: American architect Ed Tuttle was inspired by Balinese rice fields when he created this three-tiered set of infinity pools overlooking the ocean at the Amankila hotel in Bali.

LEFT: Jeweler Jean-François Fichot created this combination waterfall and fountain in his fantasy garden in Bali. OPPOSITE: Fashion designer Gianni Versace transformed his Miami Beach pool into an Italian Revival style based on his own imagination.

OPPOSITE: In Mérida, the pool at the stately Los Almendros was placed in a central courtyard to help cool the whole house. RIGHT: The 1930s Paley House pool, which was part of an estate designed by the architect Paul Williams, has an intricately detailed mosaic representing the twelve signs of the zodiac, which was created to accompany the main house by landscapist Edward Huntsman-Trout.

OPPOSITE: Antiques dealer and designer Rose Tarlow created this fantasy pool in Los Angeles to resemble a backwoods pond. RIGHT: Tony Duquette's Dawnridge is a legendary fantasy created by the designer himself. Shell-encrusted obelisks announce the entrance to the pool.

LEFT: A sublime fantasy pool at the Hartland Estate in Bali was designed by the owner with designer Ketut Sadru. OPPOSITE: Jeweler and bamboo activist John Hardy designed the Bambu Indah hotel in Bali as his vision of a tropical village. The swimming pool floats through the bungalows like a mountain stream.

OPPOSITE: A set of steps in the style of old Italian cascades forms a backdrop to the main pool area at La Loma, the main house at the Cuixmala resort in Mexico, designed by Robert Couturier. RIGHT: Hacienda Puerta Campeche is a resort hotel in Mexico's Yucatán. Here, guests can relax in outdoor hammocks over the indoor pool created out of remnants of old buildings.

LEFT: The shape of this fantasy pool at the Hartland Estate in Bali was designed to replicate the rice field it replaced. OPPOSITE: A small pool, designed by Robert Couturier, overlooks the private beach at the Cuixmala resort in Mexico.

OPPOSITE: The Morrison-Strassner circular pool house adds an element of fantasy in Palm Springs, and relates to the circular shapes of the main building. RIGHT: The Palm Springs' Abernathy House pool surround includes circular target-like sculptures by Stan Bitters. A white marble elephant is built into the pool's steps.

LEFT: One of the most successful fantasy pools in the world can be found at Hearst Castle in San Simeon. Called the Roman Pool, it is inspired by ancient Roman baths. BELOW: Neo-Greek and Roman statues decorate the Roman Pool. Here, we see Diana, Goddess of the Hunt. OPPOSITE: Tiled murals enliven a pool in Mexico's San Miguel de Allende.

LEFT: Bali's Como Shambhala hotel is built on a hillside. Architect Cheong Yew Kuan added several swimming pools to the terraces leading down the valley. OPPOSITE: In Florida's Coral Gables, this scenic backyard pool includes a waterfall and a gazebo imported from India.

LEFT: Antiques dealer and designer Rose Tarlow created this fantasy garden at her home in Los Angeles. The antique slate tiles on the gazebo roof were imported from England.
OPPOSITE: Casa Colibrí, designed by Duccio Ermenegildo for himself, includes a swimming pool with steps that lead down from the house, in Careyes, Mexico.

LEFT: The Mexican hotel Coqui Coqui, with its rough stone swimming pool, was based on the style of the ancient pyramids nearby in Coba. **BELOW**: A shallow pool runs through many of the original rooms of the Hacienda Puerta Compeche, Mexico. **OPPOSITE**: The swimming pool at the Hacienda Uayamon in Mexico was built inside the ruins of an old sisal factory.

OPPOSITE: Tirta Empul in Bali has been a sacred bathing spring since around the tenth century CE. It is an inspiration for many fantasy pools today. RIGHT: This San Miguel de Allende swimming pool includes built-in seating to socialize and cool off at the same time. The property, called the Casa Hyder, is available as a rental house. PAGE 172: The master suite's Japanese garden pool at the Como Shambhala hotel in Bali was designed by architect Cheong Yew Kuan. PAGE 173: Norm Lofthus built this natural-looking, rock-edged swimming pool to blend in with its desert surroundings in Palm Springs.

RIGHT: A swimming pool can be considered a fantasy purely based on its location. Here at the Annenberg Estate in Palm Springs, this pool overlooks a private golf course and a dream-like mountain range.

POOL ELEMENTS

A swimming pool is just as important as a house to furnish and accessorize. With the addition of spa pools and outdoor poolside kitchens, life outdoors has never been more comfortable. Catalogs offer a variety of umbrellas, daybeds, fire pits, benches, and lanterns in many sizes and shapes, as well as outdoor furniture and cushions. All-weather garden furniture, even armchairs, furnish the pool today to serve as an outdoor room, where everyone can vacation happily at home.

SPAS AND OUTDOOR SHOWERS

Originally touted for their therapeutic benefits, spas—hot tubs with heated, pulsating jets of water—have become increasingly popular since the 1960s. Candido Jacuzzi invented the pumps, jets, and filters that gave rise to the perhaps incorrect term "Jacuzzi" to describe these small heated pools often attached to a larger swimming pool. However, there are major differences. Water temperature is much hotter in a spa, between 90°F and 104°F. Since higher temperatures can cause drowsiness, most spas come with timers.

Spas and Jacuzzis don't need to be installed next to a larger pool; they can also be installed independently as a lookout to enjoy the landscape while relaxing and socializing, with perhaps a view of the ocean or a green, forested valley. Architect Manolo Mestre recently designed an iconic spa pool overlooking a river near the Mexican resort town of Valle de Bravo. As a nod to the rustic setting, Mestre included a flat rock in the step-down plateau inside the small pool, which he gave an infinity edge.

To keep the spa water clean, many people have an outdoor shower nearby, even if the pool house comes equipped with a bathroom. Washing before getting into a spa keeps the water clean, and there is nothing more pleasant than showering outdoors on a warm day. These showers can be utilitarian and incorporated into the pool design, or an opportunity for creativity. Bamboo expert and designer Linda Garland added hers to a balcony overlooking a tropical valley in Bali, and festooned it with orchids.

OPPOSITE: To take advantage of his striking Palm Springs view, Norm Lofthus built a raised spa above the swimming pool.

LEFT: Duccio Ermenegildo designed this spa pool right at the edge of the ocean in Careyes, Mexico. OPPOSITE: Dennis Gibbens created this pool and rounded gazebo, which is furnished by decorator Jamie Bush. This design makes for easy entertaining.

LEFT: Architect Manolo Mestre designed this pool and spa pool for a client in Valle de Bravo, Mexico. OPPOSITE: Michael Booth of the San Francisco firm BAMO designed this Marin County pool with an in-pool spa for the McEvoy olive ranch.

OPPOSITE: Architect Manolo Mestre carefully sited
this Jacuzzi as a place to fully enjoy this country
property in Mexico. RIGHT: Mestre also designed this
small spa pool overlooking Mexico's Valle de Bravo.

OPPOSITE: This Santa Monica hot tub by Barry Beer is separated from the pool by a sturdy glass enclosure. RIGHT: In Virginia, artist and designer Dana Westring added interest to his pool with an antique spout.

LEFT: Richard Shapiro incorporated a Moroccan-style fountain in his Malibu house courtyard. OPPOSITE: Decorator Martyn Lawrence Bullard's own pool in Hollywood sports a row of three fountain spouts. He upgraded the patio deck with tiles of his own design.

LEFT: Made Wijaya designed this outdoor shower using a Balinese pot as a showerhead for his Taman Bebek hotel. OPPOSITE, CLOCKWISE, FROM TOP LEFT: The mild climate in Los Angeles gives designer Paul Fortune's shower year-round use. Designer and bamboo enthusiast Linda Garland created an outdoor bathroom shower at Panchoran, her estate in Bali. Martyn Lawrence Bullard designed this outdoor shower at Casa Aramara in Punta Mita, Mexico. Decorator Juan Montoya provided a shower behind a stone wall in Garrison, New York.

LEFT: Barry Beer placed a shower in a secluded corner of this Santa Monica pool.
BELOW: Architect David Hertz incorporated an outdoor shower in a niche.
OPPOSITE: Martyn Lawrence Bullard added a row of water spouts to his Jacuzzi in Palm Springs.

STEPS

There are many choices of material for edging, decking, and steps. These elements add a lot to the look of the pool and help integrate it with its surroundings. Steps are usually designed to lead up to the pool and then to descend into the water. Ideally, they should be built in the same material as the pool itself. There are many types of stone, depending on what is available where the pool is being built, but it is usually chosen for its non-slip quality, as well as for its looks. Steps into the pool play an important role in the pool's design, and there are numerous points where they can be placed. At the shallow end of the pool, they can be either split into two, centrally placed, or the entire end of the pool can be stepped down in a gentle cascade.

ABOVE: Steps leading down to the Paley House pool were designed by landscapist Edward Huntsman-Trout to match the curvature of the pool. OPPOSITE: Mexican architect Manolo Mestre designed stepping stones to snake across the pool. PAGE 194: In Bali at the Como Shambhala hotel, architect Cheong Yew Kuan created formal raised tiled steps both in and out of the swimming pool. PAGE 195: Cheong Yew Kuan employed a local hardwood, an unexpected material, for steps into this pool.

EDGING

The edging of the pool, called coping, surrounds the entire pool, and is a decorative edge that covers the pool's concrete edge, often extending as decking to form a nearby patio. It provides a non-slip surface for swimmers to walk or run, and it can also be raised at some point to create seating. The choice of material depends on the style of the garden. Bunny Williams surrounded her pool with large stones found and imported from France. This gives it a rustic aspect that matches the log cabin–style Greek temple pool house.

ABOVE: At the Oscar Niemeyer Strick House in Los Angeles, river rocks skirt the edge of the pool. OPPOSITE: Designer and author Florence de Dampierre has added brightly colored furnishings and a vine-covered gazebo to her pool in Litchfield, Connecticut.

LEFT: Architect Dennis Gibbens used the same stone for the deck and the coping. BELOW: For this Los Angeles pool, the designer provides contrast in texture and color for the edging. OPPOSITE: Steven Gambrel added a small lap pool, which doubles as an ornamental pond at the back of his Sag Harbor house.

POOL HOUSES

Nothing adds more to a swimming pool than a pool house. Here, away from the constraints of the main house, this becomes a place to vacation without the inconvenience of leaving home. The structure doesn't have to be more than a roofed gazebo, but it can also be equipped like a house in miniature—with a full kitchen, bathroom, and living room. They are wonderful places to entertain friends, and often a fireplace is included for chilly evenings around a dining table overlooking the pool. Decorator and author Florence de Dampierre even added a billiard table in the pool house she designed for her family in Litchfield, Connecticut.

The thatched poolside shelters in hotels and homes in Bali are adapted from village pavilions, where they are an integral part of open family courtyards in Balinese villages. Filled with cushions, they provide an all-purpose spot to relax or eat near the pool or beach.

ABOVE: Designed by Duccio Ermenegildo, a pool house veranda overlooks the Cuixmala resort in Mexico. **OPPOSITE**: Isabel Goldsmith added a charming *palapa* (or gazebo) to her boutique hotel Las Alamandas to provide a sheltered spot to relax and enjoy her private beach.

LEFT: Josue Ramos Espinosa designed this pool house for his home in Mérida. The mirror added to the back wall gives an illusion of depth. OPPOSITE: The colorful Casa Arcadia pool house, designed by by Duccio Ermenegildo, was added to the Mexican resort Cuixmala.

LEFT: This pool in Phuket, Thailand, was built above a sheltered seating area. OPPOSITE: Architects Tichenor & Thorp in Los Angeles added a gazebo for summer entertaining at one end of their pool. PAGE 206: Collector Barry Sloane repurposed old farm buildings to create a poolside gazebo for his château in Cardet, France. PAGE 207: Martyn Lawrence Bullard furnished this pool house in Malibu as an indoor living room using all-weather fabrics.

LEFT: Architect James Dolena designed this simple, yet classically inspired, California pool house. OPPOSITE: A pool house can also include a spa area. Architect Manolo Mestre reworked an existing structure to create a peaceful outdoor room in Mérida. PAGE 210: Kristen Panitch proved that a pool house doesn't have to be big to be functional. Here, she incorporates a wicker seating group along with a small fireplace. PAGE 211: Homeowner Clora Kelly decorated the porch near the pool to serve as an outdoor living room at her Shelter Island house.

FURNISHINGS

Every poolside needs furniture to sink into and relax in the sun. A comfortable chair, chaise, or daybed greatly adds to the pleasure of being outdoors. Seating groups with outdoor coffee tables, dining tables, and chairs are the perfect way to gather and entertain friends around the pool.

While it may be tempting to recycle old outdoor furniture, the pool area will be far more harmonious if all the furnishings are in the same color and style. Ideally, they should match the look of the house. Teak furniture, aged to a pale gray, with fresh new cushions every summer is a very popular option, especially for modern-looking gardens. For traditionalists, all-weather wicker, which is virtually indestructible, can be found in both late-nineteenth-century and modern styles. To accompany them, Sunbrella fabric cushions are weatherproof and many design stores and catalogs now carry them in a wide range of colors and styles.

ABOVE: Decorator Suzanne Rheinstein upholstered her pool furniture in a fresh shade of green to complement the garden plantings. OPPOSITE: Actress Ellen Pompeo asked her designer, Martyn Lawrence Bullard, to create a comfortable place to sit by the pool. He designed this outdoor settee and added cushions covered in all-weather fabrics.

OPPOSITE: For his Connecticut home, designer Mark Silver brought in small poolside tents for extra shade.

RIGHT: At the Los Angeles Stahl House, an elegant grouping of modern garden furniture is set against a tropical landscape.

LEFT: Designer Florence de Dampierre added a chic, French-inspired metal and wood outdoor chair to her Connecticut pool furniture. **BELOW:** Decorator Suzanne Rheinstein created a corner for a table and chairs in her Los Angeles garden. **OPPOSITE:** Matthew Rolston and Ted Russell added elegant, modern outdoor furniture to their Richard Neutra–designed house in Beverly Hills.

OPPOSITE: Isabel Goldsmith's Mexican boutique resort, Las Alamandas, is enlivened by several carefully placed pool gazebos. RIGHT: A canopied daybed by Carrido Young Design in Newport Beach, California, is an ideal place to spend time by a beachside swimming pool.

LEFT: At the Palm Springs Eichler House, modern furniture adds a strong and practical element to the pool area. OPPOSITE: A hammock slung over the pool at the Hacienda Petac is a cool resting place during a hot tropical day in the Yucatán.

ACKNOWLEDGMENTS

We would like to thank all the homeowners, both old and new friends, who have let us document their private retreats and swimming pools. We have spent happy hours in many of these beautiful oases. Some homeowners have introduced us to their friends, some pools were assignments, and other friends made very helpful suggestions, including very obligingly creating splashes in their pools for us.

Special thanks to Carolyne Roehm for the use of her beautiful Connecticut pool for the cover, especially as she is the author of her own rather stunning books. Like Carolyne, we are indebted to one of the best art-directing teams in publishing today—Doug Turshen and David Huang.

We have spent many happy and inspirational hours beside designer and author Florence de Dampierre's pool, and at Isabel Goldsmith's incredibly beautiful boutique hotel, Las Alamandas, on the Costalegre coast in Mexico, near Careyes. Diane von Cranach's Puri Ganesha Homes by the Beach resort in Bali is a slice of paradise, while Realtor and collector Barry Sloane's pools, in Cardet, France, and Los Feliz in Los Angeles, are both a triumph of years of design know-how and experience.

On the East Coast, we fell in love with Juan Montoya and Urban Karlsson's creative pool design at La Formentera, their large country estate, and Bunny Williams's superbly neo-classical, rustic pool house. Simon Doonan and Jonathan Adler are keen advocates of the swimming pool lifestyle—we included two of their Shelter Island pools. Michael Bruno's Hamptons pool is also a delight. Hollister House, created by George Schoellkopf and artist Gerald Incandela, has one of the most beautiful gardens in America, with a pool cleverly disguised as an ornamental pond.

In Bali, we mourned the loss of our friend, the great tropical garden designer Made Wijaya, and included his pools at both the Villa Bebek and the Taman Bebek, as well as his pool for his family friend, restaurateur Gusky Suarsana. John Hardy and his daughter, Elora Hardy, of Ibuku in Bali, are great bamboo pioneers and masters of the rustic environment. Bud Hart drew inspiration from all these designers when he created his own tropical pool in the shape of a rice field at Hartland, his estate in Bali.

Architect Manolo Mestre is a Mexican master of resort design, and his swimming pools are timeless and extraordinary. Artist Mari Carmen Hernandez was a wonderful host when we visited her and her superb lap pool at La Meta on the Mexican coast. Both New York decorator Robert Couturier and architect Duccio Ermenegildo have designed pools for what were once Jimmy Goldsmith properties in Mexico: Robert's large swimming pool at the five-star Hacienda de San Antonio has the finest view of a volcano in the world. Both designers have contributed to Cuixmala, which is now a resort hotel near Careyes. Duccio also designed the elegant oval pool in Santo Domingo and

his own pool in Careyes, where the lovely Nicolle Meyer can often be sighted.

In the Yucatán, Reyes Rios + Larrain are the experts in converting haciendas into hotels, and they designed a beautiful pool at the Hacienda Petac, while Robert Willson and David Serrano brought in American architect Chip Bohl to create theirs in Mérida.

Longtime Sydney friends Sharyn Storrier Lyneham and Dr. Robert Lyneham conveniently finished their pool renovation just in time, while Tim was delighted to also be able to photograph another Sydney pool, with a view over the iconic Sydney Harbour for decorator Thomas Hamel.

Palm Springs, with its hot climate in summer, is all about swimming pools, and here Tim was able to photograph some of the best. Thanks to Trey Knight for his expert splash-creating dive into the Cody House pool owned by Michael Johnstone and David Zippel; while Martyn Lawrence Bullard's iconic pool is now a visual byword for Palm Springs. We are also indebted to the owner of the Abernathy House, Eric Ellenbogen, as well as Edward Cole and Chris Wigand, who own the Hearst House. We seem to be following our old friends Jim Watterson and George Martin around the world—first in Mexico, and then at the fabulous Davis House in Palm Springs with their 1950s Moroccan pool by architects Eggers and Wilkman.

In Los Angeles, two of our first friends since we arrived from London many years ago are Paul Fortune and Paul Ruscha, and we were delighted to be able to include Paul Fortune's outdoor shower and Paul Ruscha's pool in *Splash*. We have been lifetime admirers of Paul's brother, Ed Ruscha, who designed the bottom of his pool, as well as artist David Hockney, whom Tim has photographed over the years. We were also very happy to be able to include another old friend, the most talented landscape designer Nancy Goslee Power, as well as designers Suzanne Rheinstein and Richard Shapiro. Hutton Wilkinson has brilliantly restored Dawnridge, the Tony Duquette estate, and added his own touches as well. We also thank him for being able to photograph two of his own pools. Thanks to Jane Hallworth for the Ellen DeGeneres and Portia de Rossi spa, and to Liv Ballard for allowing us to photograph her beautiful Beverly Hills swimming pool. And we would also like to thank long-term architect friends like Steven Ehrlich, Brian Tichenor and Raun Thorp, Hank Koning, and Julie Eizenberg, as well as Glen Irani, Zoltan Pali, and Mark Rios.

A huge thank-you to our hardworking editor, Sandy Gilbert, our book agent, Leslie Stoker, and Tim's executive producer, Christin Markmann, who supervised the photography submission so expertly, with technical support provided by retoucher Roy Cui.

OPPOSITE: A row of small birds enjoying the infinity pool at the Hartland Estate in Bali.

First published in the United States of America
in 2019 by Rizzoli International Publications, Inc.
300 Park Avenue South
New York, New York 10010
www.rizzoliusa.com

2020 2021 2022/ 10 9 8 7 6 5 4 3 2

Printed in China

ISBN 13: 978-0-8478-6430-0

Library of Congress Control Number:
2018961286

Project Editor: Sandra Gilbert

Project Manager: Colin Hough Trapp
Editorial Assistance: Hilary Ney, Sara Pozefsky,
Rachel Selekman, and Elizabeth Smith

Art Direction: Doug Turshen with David Huang

PAGE DESCIPTIONS
HALF TITLE PAGE: The Bondi Icebergs Club ocean pool in Sydney, Australia.
TITLE PAGE: The Cody Glass House pool in Palm Springs, California.
TABLE OF CONTENTS PAGE: Le Château de Cardet, France.
ABOVE: The evening sun sets at the Las Alamandas resort in Mexico.